Schools & Scows

in

Early Sonoma

Schools & Scows
in
Early Sonoma

by George and Roger Emanuels

Sonoma Valley Historical Society

© 1998 by Roger Emanuels
ISBN 0-9607520-7-2

Sonoma, California
Published by the Sonoma Valley Historical Society
Printed in Canada

Contents

Fifty-six Years of Private Boarding Schools in Sonoma, 1853-1909
by George & Roger Emanuels

The Scows of Sonoma Creek 59
by George Emanuels

List of illustrations

Many details in this work came from the files

of the Sonoma Valley Historical Society

through the helpful assistance of the two archivists

Betty Stevens and Diane Smith.

The authors wish to make known

the assistance given them

by the several volunteers

who keep the records

in the museum history room.

Sonoma Valley Historical Society

Saint Mary's Hall was located in the Fitch House, 1853-56. At the far left in this 1860s photo, the building faces the southwest corner of the plaza.

Saint Mary's Hall

For much of the 1850s Sonoma residents sloshed through the muddy mire of the town's streets in winter, and in summer they stepped over the crusty, dry ruts and potholes created by horses and wagon wheels.

Women and girls in their long skirts avoided walking outside whenever possible in wet weather and in summer held their dresses higher as they walked across dusty streets.

There was plenty to do at home. Boys worked with their fathers, laboring on the farm or tending store. Girls cared for the home, helping their mothers with the never ending household chores. Dusting, washing, preparing food and feeding the chickens monopolized their time.

Teachers who came to California in the early fifties found there was no public school system, though there were some church schools. For many children, the only school was at home. Wealthy families might hire a teacher to live with the family. In Contra Costa County, the renowned storyteller Bret Harte found his first employment as a tutor with a rancher at remote Tassajara.

In Sonoma, General Mariano Vallejo had hired Don Frederika Reger in 1849 as tutor for his children. Reger lived in the two-story adobe residence facing the plaza. Known then as "La Casa Grande", the first floor was occupied by the tutor, two doctors, and a military authority. The Vallejo family lived on the second floor.[1]

The first American school in Sonoma is described by Eliza Donner Houghton, a survivor of the Donner Party in 1846. In 1849 she lived with Mr. and Mrs. Christian Brunner and later wrote about attending the first school in Sonoma.

> The school room was a dreary adobe, containing two rows of benches so high that when seated we could barely touch the earthen floor with our toes.[2]

By 1853 General Vallejo was a state senator. He continued to be concerned about the education of his daughters, and arranged for Rev. J.L. Ver Mehr to come to Sonoma from San Francisco to teach the children.

Ver Mehr was an Episcopal clergyman who had come to San Francisco in 1849. He gained a following of some note and had established Grace Chapel. Vallejo met the preacher and found him willing to consider changing his home to a placid country town. In addition, Vallejo offered the use of

Sonoma Valley Historical Society

An undated photo of the Fitch adobe., probably around 1860. It sits on the corner of First Street West and Napa Street. The Plaza is to the right. The ground floor is of adobe, and the second floor is wood frame.

his large home in Sonoma for a school.

Ver Mehr arrived in Sonoma in August 1853 with his wife and several children. Upon calling on Vallejo, the reverend learned to his amazement that the senator had withdrawn his offer of his home for the new school.

Not completely discouraged by the turn of events Ver Mehr rented the Fitch home, an adobe on First Street West in the block facing the plaza.

On September 1, 1853, Ver Mehr began operating Saint Mary's Hall for Young Ladies. However, he continued to perform church services and visit with parishioners in San Francisco. Every two weeks he took the stage to Lakeville where he met the steamer from Petaluma which landed him in San Francisco three hours later.

> Dr. Ver Mehr's school at the time was the finest educational establishment north of San Francisco.[3]

The Episcopal minister hadn't been in Sonoma very long before he heard the story which had caused the general to withdraw the offer he had made to Ver Mehr when he first met the man.

It seemed that Vallejo, now a state senator, had overestimated his abilities. In the desire to appear more important than he was in the eyes of the newly elected fellow legislators, he made an offer designed to move the state capitol from San Jose to a new town of Vallejo where he owned thousands of acres. He proposed to donate 156 acres for the town and $370,000, of which $125,000 he specified was for the construction of a capitol building. In making the offer Vallejo undoubtedly had in mind the increase in value of his remaining land.

The legislators moved to the new town for their next session only to find the expected capitol building was not yet built. In fact, the lumber which the general ordered had not been delivered.

Accustomed to his daily needs being supplied by his staff of servants and craftsmen at his Petaluma adobe, Vallejo suddenly found himself in need of tens of thousands of dollars to fulfill the overly generous commitments he had made to his fellow legislators. His head swirling with the difficulties he was in, he called off the few obligations he could. One of those was the suggestion he made to the Episcopal minister to establish a school in his home in Sonoma. His lack of business tact and his inability to sell enough land for cash meant his offer to Ver Mehr had to be withdrawn.

Before long, however, Vallejo again changed his mind and invited the Saint Mary's Hall into his Casa Grande on the plaza.

In 1856, the Ver Mehrs' nine children ranged in age from 3 to 13. One day in November, five-year old Bella complained of a sore throat. Her father later wrote about the incident:

> Diphtheria was then making sad havoc through the whole country. The physician was called; an able man, but unacquainted with the disease then coming as a scourge over many families. He applied the only remedy, a caustic, to the throat, but in an inefficient manner.

In spite of treatment, she died on November 20, and three more daughters succumbed in the next eight days. Some days later he accompanied the remains of his daughters to San Francisco.

> I placed the four coffins on two wagons. Following in a buggy, with my eldest son, we went to Lakeville, where, at ten o'clock, we stood on the wharf, expecting the steamer.

He took them for burial at Lone Mountain Cemetery in San Francisco. Discouraged and in need of a change, the surviving Ver Mehr family returned to San Francisco almost immediately. Local churches raised funds to help them get a new start in the city, and Saint Mary's Hall reopened on the corner of Geary and Powell streets in January, 1857. The minister later reported, "Many of our old pupils rejoined us there." The school was moved to a Bush Street address where fire destroyed it in 1859.[4]

Beaten again, in November, 1859 Ver Mehr moved his

family to Napa Valley, where he purchased fifteen acres which he called La Lomita. They raised chickens and vegetables, tended a vineyard and made some wine. The Reverend continued to preach at church each Sunday in Napa and occasionally in Spanish at San Quentin Prison.[5] He died in 1886 at the age of 77.

Notes

[1] Robert D. Parmelee, *Pioneer Sonoma*, Sonoma: The Sonoma Valley Historical Society, 1972, appendix p.121.

[2] Eliza P. Donner Houghton, *The expedition of the Donner party and its tragic fate*, Los Angeles: Grafton Publishing Corp., 1920; University of Nebraska Press, 1997, p.223.

[3] Marion Shaw Sneyd-Kynnersley, "Stories I have heard of Los Guilicos", typwritten manuscript, Sonoma Valley Historical Society.

[4] J.L. Ver Mehr, *A Checkered Life*, San Francisco: A. L. Bancroft and Co. 1877.

[5] Madie Brown, "Reverend Doctor Ver Mehr", in *The Academy Scrapbook*, Vol I (April 1951) No. 10, p. 296-306. Courtesy Sonoma Valley Historical Society.

Sonoma Valley Historical Society

In December 1858 the Cumberland Presbyterian Church bought Salvador Vallejo's one-story adobes on the corner of Spain Street and First Street West. Soon the trustees hired two carpenters to add the second floor, containing 48 dormitory rooms.

Cumberland College

One year after the departure of the Ver Mehr family, the Cumberland Presbyterian Church established a school in Sonoma in December 1857. It first occupied the Salvador Vallejo adobe buildings on the west side of the plaza, serving area students and boarding students. Seven years later, in 1864, the school moved to a location on Broadway, where it continued for nine more years. It ceased operation in 1873.[1]

Sonoma in the 1850s had not exhibited much progress. Agriculture was not significant, and the town seemed to be in an economic backwater. Its importance as a military garrison was gone, now that California was firmly in the United States. General Vallejo's dream of founding the state capitol at a nearby location failed when Sacramento was designated the capitol.

Sonoma was considered a dilapidated remnant of the Mexican period in California by one reporter from the *San*

Francisco Alta, who wrote rather condescendingly,

> The suburbs of the city have a far more lively ap-
> pearance than the plaza, and indeed the latter is
> one of the dullest places in existence. You might
> believe yourself, when looking at it, in some vil-
> lage like Durango or Chihuahua, although some
> of the late wooden ornaments to the clumsy adobe
> houses have too much of a clipper build for the
> Mexican notions. A few persons may be seen
> lounging under the corridors, either asleep or play-
> ing draughts, and except for these or an occasional
> mounted Spaniard or a Missourian driving an ox
> team, there is seldom anyone to be seen.[2]

Another blow occurred in 1854 when the county seat was
moved from Sonoma to Santa Rosa. A.J. Cox, editor of the
Sonoma Bulletin commented on the removal,

> Departed - Last Friday the County officers with
> the archives left town... We are only sorry that they
> did not take the courthouse along — not because
> it would be an ornament to Santa Rosa, but because
> its removal would have embellished our plaza...
> No more do we see county lawyers and loafers in
> general, lazily engaged in the laudable effort of
> whittling under the veranda posts, which, by the
> way, required little more to bring the whole fabric
> to the ground... The courthouse is deserted, like
> some feudal castle, only tenented, perhaps, by bats,
> rats, and fleas.[3]

The plaza presented a forlorn appearance, treeless and
unkempt. Untethered cows and horses decorated the dirt

streets and paths with manure droppings. Buzzing flies and stench permeated the air of downtown Sonoma in the hot days of summer. Here and there an untied cow grazed, dogs lay scratching fleas, and chickens clucked and crowed. An ugly ditch crossed the square, and a cannon wheel lay over it to serve as a foot bridge.[4]

> It was a common sight to see heavy clumsy wagons drawn by oxen six or eight of them dragging heavy loads through the main streets of Sonoma. A heavy cloud of dust followed them all through town and down Broadway to the Embarcadero.[5]

The need for a school was self-evident. Saint Mary's Hall had ceased to function at the end of 1856 with the departure of the Ver Mehr family. The State of California had formed the State Board of Education in 1851, but no public schools were available locally until the boards of supervisors of Sonoma and Mendocino Counties established a district in 1857. At that time about 250 children lived in Sonoma Valley. Four public schools opened for classes that year, three in the surrounding areas of Ash Springs, Dunbar, Watmaugh, and one in the Methodist Church in downtown Sonoma. In December, another school, Sonoma Academy, was opened by the Cumberland Presbyterian Church.

In 1844, General Vallejo's brother Salvador had employed the mission Indians to extract earth from the plaza to make adobe bricks for the construction of three one-story buildings on his property at the corner of First Street West and Spain Street, facing the northwest corner of the plaza. He expected to rent the buildings as a meeting hall for the newly established mayor and town council, and commercial purposes (photo, page 8).

Only the adobe known as La Casita survives today, a private residence facing Spain Street. The others were at the current 415 First Street West, separated by a passageway from the L-shaped building on the corner, which had a wing facing Spain Street. The passageway led to an open corral in the back. Shortly after construction, this corner adobe was converted into a theater called The Colonnade. The one-story gallery on its north side suggested the name. It became the El Dorado Hotel in 1849.

The entire complex was occupied by the Cumberland Presbyterian Church in December 1857 as the Sonoma Academy.

The Cumberland Presbyterian Church got its beginning in the Cumberland area of Virginia and Tennessee and soon spread throughout the southern states. It was one of many evangelical Protestant denominations which discovered new ground to sow in the emerging frontier society of gold rush California.

The Cumberland Presbyterian Church in California was

organized April 4, 1851 in Santa Clara County, by the Reverends John H. Braly, Cornelius Yager, Wesley Gallimore, James M. Small and Licentiate John M. Cameron.

After holding a camp meeting near Napa in 1852, Rev. Small met with others in Sonoma and secured money to build a church. The Pacific Presbytery was organized in the house of Rev. Cameron in 1854. It was this organization which established the Sonoma Academy toward the end of 1857.[6] Similar schools were founded at Alamo and Stockton at about the same time.

John Braly was the founding president of the school and Rev. Y.A. Anderson became president in 1860. Soon a second floor was added to each of the adobes facing the plaza, joined by a vestibule. To accommodate boarders, forty-three rooms were created on the upper floor. "Young ladies from the best families came to Sonoma to be educated."[7]

Seventy-six male and female students were enrolled in 1860 at the "two-story adobe building"[8]

Ninety-nine students were enrolled in 1860-61. Fifty-two were boys of which only fourteen were boarders. Of the forty-six girls, ten were boarders. The school year began on July 16 and ended May 1.[9]

Boarders paid $4.50 per week plus $1.00 for laundry. In the male department, science courses cost $30, and higher preparatory studies cost $20 to $30. Language classes cost

Sonoma Valley Historical Society

This 1860s photo looks across the northwest acrossthe plaza. Cumberland College, formerly the El Dorado Hotel, occupies the two-story building on the far right.

$10 per session.

In the female department, preparatory studies fees were $15 for the first session and $20 for the second. Collegiate courses cost $25 for the junior class, $30 for the middle class and $35 for the senior class.

Charges were made for the use of the piano, and extra costs were incurred in the embroidery, drawing, painting, French, and Spanish classes. A janitor fee of $2 per half session was added, and students paid extra for the candles they used. Families were notified in advance,

> There will be a public examination, ending on the Friday of the last week of each session...and no students will be advanced unless such promotion be merited.

By 1861 the name of the school was changed from Sonoma Academy to Cumberland College.[10] The school catalog for the year ending May 1, 1861 lists the board of trustees as Rev. Y.A. Anderson, president; S.B. Bright, secretary; G.M. McConnell, treasurer; Rev. C.H. Crawford, agent; W.C. Wallace, Esq.; Maj. John H. Seawell; C.W. Ish; Nathaniel Jones; Rev. E.P. Henderson; R. Moore; W.M.A. Townsend; Capt. G.P. Swift; D.C. Rupe; and John H. Braly, A.B., member exofficio.

The faculty is given as J.H. Braly, A.B., president and professor of mental and moral philosophy and belles lettres;

Rev. A. Grigsby, A.M., professor of mathematics; Rev. William N. Cunningham, A.B., professor of languages; Rev. A.W. Sweeney, principal, and teacher in the female department; Miss Octavia S. Kenney, teacher of piano music, embroidery, drawing and painting.

The catalog continues to list the faculty for the fall 1861 term.

> Our president, John H. Braly, A.B., having resigned on account of ill health, and Rev. A.W. Sweeney called to the Presidency of Columbia College, Oregon, and Rev. A. Grigsby, A.M., removed to Texas, the following faculty has been chosen for the coming session by the board: Rev. William N. Cunningham, A.B., president, and professor of mental and moral philosophy and belles lettres; J.C. Ewing, A.B., professor of mathematics; Rev. E.P. Henderson, A.M., professor of languages; Miss Octavia S. Kenney, principal of the female department, and teacher of piano music, embroidery, drawing and painting.

Students are reported to have come from San Jose, San Francisco, Grass Valley, Round Valley (Mendocino County), Sonora, Santa Clara, Lafayette, Mark West Creek, Cache Creek, Nevada and Stockton.

John Braly later moved to southern California where he invested in real estate. The town of Brawley was named for him, the change of spelling probably reflecting the pronunciation of the name.

Trustee Crawford later wrote of his early impression of the town of Sonoma,

> A beautiful country to look at but rather a hard place for a poor man to make a living. In my judgment there were better locations for a denominational college than this one, and one where it would have prospered and done great good. A wine producing country such as Sonoma was then, and still more so in after years, was by no means favorable for the morals of the youth who lived there.[11]

Rev. William Cunningham had come to California in December 1859 after completing his studies at Cumberland University in Lebanon, Tennessee. He first came to Stockton to minister to the Cumberland Presbyterian Church. His greatest contribution came however, as a teacher and president at the Cumberland College in Sonoma. He had come to the college to teach, and now as the nation headed toward Civil War, he found himself in the position of president of the College. In this era fights broke out among youngsters from the north and south of the eastern United States.[12]

One of the early students who later became a teacher in the college was Daniel Edwin Bushnell. Born in 1841 in Cadiz, Ohio, his parents moved to Adair County, Ohio when he was still a youth. Most of his early schooling was acquired by attending a nearby Cumberland Presbyterian

Church.

Bushnell arrived in California in the spring of 1859, with the intention of preaching for his church. He first made contact with old friends and acquaintances, visiting Y.A. Anderson in Sonoma, and others in St. Helena. He soon established his home in Stockton, and later in the Tassajara region of Contra Costa County.

With barely time to settle in, Bushnell returned to Sonoma on April 27, 1859 to attend a meeting of the Pacific Presbytery of the old school Cumberland Presbyterian Church. In his diary he describes the 24-hour journey, leaving Stockton by steamer in the afternoon. He disembarked at Benicia where he stayed the night. The next day he continued by stage to Sonoma, arriving at 3:15 in the afternoon. He first stopped at the Union Hotel, which he considered a

> rather unpleasant place. Cool, no fire. Drinking and gambling going on.[13]

Bushnell became a student at Cumberland College in 1862, and was impressed with Cunningham's leadership..

> It was here at Sonoma, in the old adobe building occupied as a boarding school and church, that the writer first met President Cunningham and had the honor of his noble friendship for four years in the relation of pupil and assistant in the work of instruction. This was in 1862 the second year per-

haps of President Cunningham's connection with the College. The school was well attended and had an extended influence. A large number of young ladies and gentlemen were here prepared for their life work. But the labor required to maintain the enterprise was prodigious. A debt of $7,000 was against the property, the adobe and the nearly completed foundation for a new building, both being mortgaged to secure the debt. In due time the debt was provided for and a joint stock company was organized which secured the erection of the new building at a cost of $12,000 to which the school was at once transferred. But the wine interest had by this time so completely changed the character of the population and surrounding of the beautiful valley of Sonoma as to make it impossible to maintain a college enterprise there. And hence the work of years was abandoned. The beautiful concrete building is now (1897) owned by the School Department of the town and occupied by the High School of the place and is still one of the most conspicuous land marks in this famous old "Valley of the Moon".[14]

During his years in Sonoma, Bushnell often walked to neighboring communities to preach on Sundays, and one source refers to him as the "boy-preacher". He drew a loyal following at the Wolfskill ranch, on the bank of Putah Creek in Solano County. Sarschel Wolfskill was a fellow Missourian, and gave generously to the Cumberland cause in California. His children were boarding students at Cumberland College. Bushnell was accustomed to walking the sixty-miles from Sonoma, and helped organize a church there. On the first anniversary of the church in 1863, Bushnell hurried to deliver a promised sermon. About half way through his journey he reached Fairfield and realized he would not be able to arrive in time at the church. So he spent his precious five dollars on a livery rig. That evening he delivered his sermon to an audience of faithful who packed the school house at Wolfskill. Not wanting to pay for a second day of rental on his horse and buggy, he immediately returned the rig to Fairfield. He was then faced with the return to Sonoma on foot, more than thirty miles away, accomplished all in one day.[15]

Dr. E.D. Walker brought his family to Sonoma about 1860 from their home on the Mokelumne River. His office was on First Street West, about a block from the plaza, across from the Methodist Church.[16] Walker was a physician from Tennessee who had tried his luck at farming in San Joaquin County and mining in Calaveras County since arriving overland in California with his family in 1849.

His children were students at Cumberland College, and among his few papers is found a literary magazine, *The Academy Echoes*, a collection of essays and riddles. This April 1863 collection is on pages 20 cm. wide and 31 cm. high. There is a title page, 11 pages of handwritten text, and a blank end sheet. The pages are lightly ruled, and are embossed in the upper left corner with an oval and small writing. A large watermark includes the word "Windsor". The

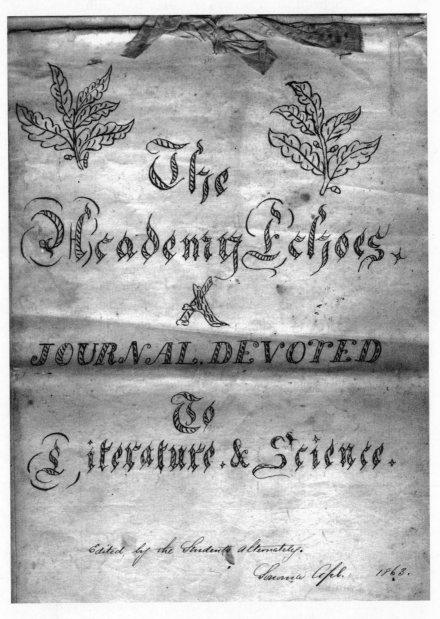

M.L. Parsons Davis collection

"The Academy Echoes, A Journal Devoted to Literature & Science. Edited by the students alternately. Sonoma Apl. 1863."

pages each have a hole at the top center, through which they are bound with a simple silk ribbon. The title page contains crude but elaborate decorative writing and drawings of two leaves. Brown ink is used throughout, and all appears to be in the same hand. There are a few corrections in pencil. The texts are compositions by students at the Cumberland College in 1863.

The title page reads

The Academy Echoes
A Journal Devoted To Literature & Science
Edited, by the Students alternately.
Sonoma Apl. 1863

The introduction reveals that the writer did not excel at spelling.

Editorial
Kind friends and dear schoolmates we now present you with the first number of the college Echoes for the twelfth session of our school. We feel that the duty is an ardious one, and that we are incompetent to take such a responcibility upon ourselves as we consider the first Editorial and presentation of our beloved paper to be. But we assure you that [unreadable] labor [unreadable] shall be spared upon our part. To make the paper worthy of your consideration, we have selected of the choicest matter both of Literature Learning and science and other good things connected with the Cumberland College. The popularity and high standing of your former editors who so well merit [unreadable] has

stimulated us to use every exertion to give you a paper, which if smaller in size for want of contribution at this the beginning of our school shall lack nothing in the way of matter.

Student Joseph Hayne wrote one paragraph he titled "The mines".

The mining interests are breaking out every where and many a poor fellows have gone to try their luck and some of them make there fortune while others work and toil but get nothing, but sickness and death for their labor. At first a great many people went but after they had been there a few months packed up their bundles and put off for home. There has been a great many deaths since the mines were discovered from the fallings of banks drinking unholesome water I believe this valley is about the pleasantest in California.

Lilburn Boggs came to Sonoma with his wife, and his oldest son and his wife in 1847 from Missouri. General Vallejo had been helpful to them on their arrival, so when the younger Boggs family had their first child, he was named after the general. Cumberland student Guadalupe Vallejo Boggs was one of the first Americans to be born in California, and is represented by more than one essay in the collection.

Walker's children were attending Cumberland College in the spring of 1864 when Henrietta died of scarlet fever, according to the April 2, 1864 issue of the Napa County

Register. Her younger brother Willie died about two weeks later. The following appeared in the Cumberland church newspaper, the *Presbyter*.

> Obituaries
> Tribute of Respect
> We, the undersigned, appointed by the President of the College to draft resolutions expressive of the feelings and sentiments of the students, in regard to the death of our worthy friend and schoolmate, Miss Henrietta C. Walker, who departed this life at her father's residence in Sonoma, Friday, March 25th, 1864, would submit the following resolutions: Whereas it has pleased Almighty God to remove from time to eternity our dear friend and school-mate Miss Henrietta C. Walker, be it resolved, that this school received with deep emotions the melancholy intelligence of the death of our respected schoolmate, and view her loss as a severe calamity to the school, and to society, of which she was a brilliant ornament.
> *Resolved*, That we tender to the family and friends of our departed fellow-schoolmate, our sincere sympathies and unfeigned regret at her untimely demise.
> *Resolved*, That the College Echoes be draped in mourning, and that a copy of these resolutions be sent to the family, and also to the *Presbyter* for publication.
> James I. McConnell, Henry Z. Morris, Miss Mary Hendreson, Miss Marcelona Smith, Miss Jennie Martin.
> For the *Presbyter*.
>
> Death Reigns
> Dear *Presbyter*: Will you please chronicle in your columns the very sudden departure from earth, on Wednesday, April 6th, of our young friend and schoolmate, Willie E. Walker. He was prepared to

start for school on the previous day, and before
school closed on the 7th he was "cold in death."
The tears of mourning had not been dried which
his sister's death had caused to flow. The fond
parents' heart string had not ceased to vibrate with
sorrow, ere they are again touched by the afflict-
ing hand of Divine Providence. Surely with *seven*
dear voices swelling the music of heaven from one
household, it must have many attractions to the
few who remain. A generous community are full
of sympathy for the parents and kindred so sadly
bereaved; and I know, dear reader, you will join
with us in devoutly commending them to the love
of that great and good Being. "Who tempereth the
winds to the shorn lamb," and encourage them to
look beyond these scenes of death and pain, to one
all cloudless and pure, where death *cannot* come.
D.E. Bushnell
Cumberland College
Apr. 7th, 1864[17]

The school was moved to a new location in the fall of
1864. The new college building on Broadway was an attractive three-story structure with full basement, capped by a
handsome mansard roof. It was short lived, however, and
the school doors were closed about 1873. The new University of California in Berkeley probably attracted many of
the students away from Sonoma. Some objected to the school
being located in an area where the wine industry was so
prominent.

The fine cement building remained vacant for a number
of years. On July 29, 1891 the Board of Education agreed to
lease the building for $4 per month and took an option to

Sonoma Valley Historical Society

Cumberland Presbyterian College, about 1864. The building was leased by the Sonoma Valley Union High School from 1891 until it was damaged in the 1906 earthquake. The stone foundation still remains at 870 Broadway.

buy it for $2,500 in order to locate the high school there.

On April 18, 1906 the Great Earthquake which killed about 50 people in Santa Rosa, buckled some of the walls of the school. Subsequent examination determined that the building was not fit to be occupied. The cement structure was torn down and replaced with a frame building of the same dimension and three stories in height. The high school held classes here until 1916.

The original stone foundation, undisturbed by the 1906 and subsequent earthquakes, sits today as a reminder of the glory of the structure, possibly the most attractive nonresidential building in the city of Sonoma.

Schools and Scows in Early Sonoma

Notes

[1] Rev. D.E. Bushnell, D.D. "Rev. William Newton Cunningham, A.M., a character sketch", *Alabama Cumberland Presbyterian*. Piedmont, Alabama, March 1, 1897, no. 4. Bushnell writes that in 1861 Rev. Cunningham "accepted the presidency of Cumberland College at Sonoma where he remained for a period of twelve years." There is no further reference to the school, and so is presumed that it ceased operations at the end of that 12-year period, about 1873.

[2] Robert D. Parmelee, *Pioneer Sonoma*, Sonoma: The Sonoma Valley Historical Society, 1972, p.101.

[3] ibid.

[4] Edna Cooper, "General Vallejo's Plaza" in *Saga of Sonoma*, Sonoma: The Sonoma Valley Historical Society, 1976.

[5] Marion Shaw Sneyd-Kynnersley, "Stories I have heard of Los Guilicos", typwritten manuscript, Sonoma Valley Historical Society.

[6] *The Pacific*, Vol. 6, No. 51, Dec. 10, 1857, p.2 col. 3.

[7] Celeste Murphy, *People of the Pueblo*, Sonoma: W.L. and C.G. Murphy, 1937, pp.162-163.

[8] William Warren Ferrier, *Ninety Years of Education in California 1846-1936*, Berkeley: Sather Gate Book Shop, 1937.

[9] *Catalogue of Cumberland College (formerly Sonoma Academy) for the Collegiate Year Ending May 1, 1861*, published by Presbyter Print, Alamo. Bancroft Library.

[10] Clifford M. Drury, "Church-Sponsored Schools in Early California", *Pacific Historian*, vol. 20, no. 2.

[11] Rev. Charles Howard Crawford, *Scenes of Earlier Days in Crossing the Plains to Oregon and Experiences of Western Life*, 1898, Petaluma. Reprint 1962, Quadrangle Books, Chicago, pp.88 ff.

[12] Clara Johnson, "Pioneer Schools" in *Saga of Sonoma*, Sonoma: The Sonoma Valley Historical Society, 1976, p.14.

[13] Daniel E. Bushnell's papers and diaries are at the San Francisco Theological Seminary in San Anselmo, California.

[14] Bushnell diaries.

[15] ibid.

[16] Edna Cooper, "Pioneer Physicians" in *Saga of Sonoma*, Sonoma: The Sonoma Valley Historical Society, 1976, p.19.

[17] This newspaper clipping is glued to a page in a scrapbook of E.D. Walker's granddaughter, Kate Parsons, authors' family collection.

Locust Grove School

Amelia Barbara Sother was born in 1831 in Kent, England, and first came to Staten Island, New Jersey with her family. When she was 16 years old she said good-bye to her parents, and carrying aboard her bags, she stepped up the gangplank of a sailing ship destined for San Francisco. The year was 1847 or 1848.[1]

She felt strengthened by the story about another native of Kent, William A. Richardson, who owned more than thirty square miles north of San Francisco Bay. The arrival of the 27 year-old sailor in California in 1822 was legendary. He had been first mate of the whaler *Orion* when he deserted his ship at Yerba Buena Cove.[2]

Aided by the mission padres at Mission Dolores, the sailor made an application, in Spanish, to the Governor at Monterey, to be allowed to remain in California. The request met with approval subject to the condition that he be willing to teach navigation and carpentry whenever requested.

While waiting for the official decision, Richardson built a boat for himself, small but adequate for service on San Francisco Bay. The tools he used were his which he had carried on the whaler.

Apparently his boat was the best to carry heavy loads. The missionaries asked him in 1823 to deliver a bell, newly arrived from Mexico for the new outpost at Sonoma.

Amelia heard that he had married the daughter of the presidio commandante in the Bay of San Francisco, Don Ignacio Martinez, and then petitioned Governor Alvarado for a grant of land. He received 19,751 acres of southern Marin County.

At where he called Whaler's Cove, now Sausalito, he sold fresh water, firewood, and fresh beef. He had plenty of help from the local Indians in cutting wood and in the slaughter of cattle. He and his bride settled at the *hacienda* he had built on his El Rancho de Sausalito.[3]

Richardson was prosperous and an important figure in early California. In 1837 Governor Figueroa named him Port Captain of San Francisco Bay.

Back home in Kent, people found it hard to believe the stories they heard from sailors who passed through San Francisco. By the time they came to the United States, Amelia and her parents were probably very familiar with the exotic accounts of Richardson and of distant California.

She had been surprised and excited by stories in the New York papers of some thirty or so Americans who had captured the Mexican military commander of Alta California. She read in amazement about the United States naval officers who helped bring down the Mexican flag at Monterey, and who took part in establishing a new U.S. territory. Amelia Sother sailed to where many considered would become the next state to join the Union.

The ship headed south and with favorable winds navigated the Straits of Magellan. Then it headed north along the coast of south America, toward the 38th north parallel. Ultimately the ship and its passengers arrived safely in a timely fashion in San Francisco.

The town of San Francisco offered few amenities in 1848. It was a tent city, with most people living in houses which contained muslin for the outside walls. At night people sought out the gambling houses for light and warmth, as neither was available where they roomed. People were friendly. Everyone whom Amelia met was also a recent arrival, some coming from as far away as Europe. Young ladies were so few in San Francisco that year that those who were there were treated as royalty. Men tipped their hats whether they were acquainted with the passing lady or not.

One young man who paid special attention was one of

the few medical men in town. Dr. Baxter showed Amelia such deference and respect that when he proposed marriage, she accepted. They married and sailed south for their honeymoon.[4]

Amelia became pregnant on the trip. While in a south American port the doctor contracted a disease, and they returned to San Francisco. Baxter never regained his health, and died soon after. The baby died at birth.

At about this time gold was discovered at Coloma, in the foothills east of Sacramento. As the news spread, the rush was on.

When a few men came back from the hills showing off their bags of nuggets and gold dust, nearly every able bodied man in town grabbed a pick, shovel and gold pan, and rushed away.

On top of widowhood and loss of her baby, Amelia now faced a town gone wild. That first year tens of thousands of men scrambled their way to the hills, eager to make camp alongside their El Dorado. They bought up supplies of all kinds. Store shelves remained empty of many supplies until the next ship arrived with what was needed.

If they arrived by ship in San Francisco, men stayed only long enough to equip themselves before heading to the interior and the gold fields. While Amelia faced the trials of living alone in the hastily built town of 1849, little did she know that the man who would shape her destiny was on his way from China.[5]

He was Charles W. Lubeck, a Swedish sea captain born in 1814. He was skipper of his own vessel, and had delivered a cargo of manufactured goods to China. He made some profitable trades, and expected to retire there. However, when news of the gold discovery reached China, he was ready to make the trip to California, and at the age of 36 Lubeck came to San Francisco. In 1850 so many ships filled the harbor that he was forced to anchor out on the rim beyond hundreds of deserted vessels.

Lubeck did not go to the mines, and somehow had the ability to purchase land immediately upon arrival. And it was not long before he married the widow Amelia Sother. The year was 1851, and California had become a state barely a year earlier.

San Francisco was a lawless city. The "hounds", a thieving group of hoodlums from Australia, were making the city their playground. They stole, blackmailed, and murdered with impunity. Corrupt police accepted bribes to look the other way. Few hounds or police were ever prosecuted for these activities.

A major fire swept over the city, destroying dwellings and stores alike.

In the spring of 1851, Amelia and Charles Lubeck decided to leave San Francisco and considered moving to Sonoma, then a county seat. Perhaps business could be recorded quicker there. Maybe it could be a bit easier. He would go there and see if any good land could be bought on terms which he could afford.

On his first trip to Sonoma he liked what he saw. Good soil for growing crops was available at prices which were sure to rise. He saw the land in April, the most favorable month of the year there. The hills and valley floors were all green.

On April 14, 1851, Charles Lubeck bought 31 acres on lower Broadway. He had a cottage constructed on the property and the couple moved from San Francisco to Sonoma in May, 1852. On August 24, 1852 he purchased 51 acres on the east side of Broadway, adjacent to the first property.[6] A fruit orchard was planted on this second property.

Indeed, Sonoma was a busy place then. The courthouse on the plaza was bustling, with lawyers coming and going, arms full of papers.

The sea captain received the appointments he had applied for. Sweden, Norway, and Denmark each appointed him consul. Along with the new posts came a request from a Swedish manufacturer that Lubeck become its agent. He would represent a company that constructed houses with wooden pegs rather than with nails. The houses would be sent by ship to San Francisco. Lubeck would show sketches of the houses to prospective buyers, take their order, and earn a commission on each sale. He subsequently placed an order for five such houses which arrived on the ship *Sarah*.

Mr. and Mrs. Lubeck found a place in Sonoma society.[7] They were different from many people, having arrived in California by ship. Many in town were from Mexican families or had trudged across the plains.

Amelia Lubeck, an eighteen year-old in search of adventure in 1848, had gained a confidence within three years that gave her a lively and keen outlook on life. She must have been an exciting guest at any social gathering. And her husband was a world traveler with the knowledge and memories of sailing from Europe to Asia, having lived for a short time in China.

In September, 1852 Lubeck bought 192 acres of good farm land from Thomas O. Larkin to the east but near the 82 acres he bought in 1851.[8] He made this purchase in his business name, Lubeck & Company, and paid $22 per acre ($4,000). One month later he transferred title to the 82 acres to his wife.

Not satisfied with a farming life, Lubeck found little to keep him alert. And the loss of the county seat in 1854 was a blow which turned his attention back to San Francisco. He returned there and resumed working under the name

Lubeck & Co.

At work he acted as a ship broker and lumber broker.[9] He sold logs or lumber to mills in San Francisco. He earned a commission on the deliveries to the mills and also another commission on the ship he chartered to make the deliveries. In this atmosphere the former shipmaster felt at home.

In these maritime activities, Lubeck borrowed substantial sums from the San Francisco Bank. A year later, unfortunately he was unable to meet his obligation when due. When pressed for repayment, the former sea captain surrendered his 180 acres in Sonoma.

Lubeck found himself at an ebb tide in his life with all his accumulated assets gone and no real estate in his name. His depressed state forced him to do the only thing he was equipped to do. He went back to sea.[10]

Amelia felt the loss for a while but turned to the good things around her. Her orchard produced heavy crops of fruit and her gardens were bountiful. Her cottage was in good repair. And she was in good health.

In 1869 she received the tragic news of the death of both her sister and brother-in-law in Australia. Sadly they left behind eight children.[11]

Amelia acted on her first instinct. Her inbred generous nature led her to quickly reply, "Send them all to me and I will make a home for them."

The eight orphans eventually reached Sonoma in 1869. The oldest, a girl of eighteen, then returned to Australia to be married. The remaining seven siblings were known as the Landsborough children. They fell in love with their benefactress and her country home. Amelia hired a tutor to oversee their schooling.

They called Amelia "Auntie Lubeck". This name was later used by scores of children who came to live with her.

About a year after the Landsborough children arrived, neighbor Mrs. Tilden died.[12] She left three children, Bessie, Leslie, and Charles. For several reasons Mr. Tilden could not make a home for them. Amelia not only took them in but formally adopted all three. As if those ten children were not enough, Amelia took in three more orphans. They were Nora, Beatrice, and Fred Bioletti, and "lived there during their younger days."

There was an obvious need for housing for thirteen children. So Amelia designed a two-story building with a boys' dormitory on the upper floor. The first floor would provide a school room, kitchen, and dining space. A new cottage would be for the girls. Four-hole outhouses were located in back.

In 1871 women lacked many of the privileges taken for granted today. They could not vote. And most important to Amelia, they could not buy, sell, or obligate real estate. The

Locust Grove School 1885
Schellville, Sonoma County, California

Mrs. A. B. Lubeck, Principal   Miss Georgy Landsborough, Music Teacher
Miss Bella Landsborough, Drawing Teacher   Emil Pohli, General Teacher

left to right:
Leslie Tilden (Mrs. Bidwell of Baltimore)
Georgy Landsborough
Bella Landsborough
Miss Lily Harrison (daughter of Mrs. Sother)
Etna Sterret (student)
C.W. Lubeck (husband of Mrs. A. Lubeck, retired Swedish sea captain)
Tom Landsborough (about four)
Mrs. L.M. Landsborough
Leonard M. Landsborough holding Lucile
two students in background
Amy Landsborough in buggy
Bessie Tilden left of buggy (Mrs. Ridell)
Margaret Williams seated right of buggy, student, sister of J. Williams
Mrs. A.B. Lubeck
Mr. T. Sother, her father
Mrs. Sother
Frank C. Mortimer, seated on ground
Emil Pohli, teacher
Nicholas ten Bosch Jr., with spade
Amy Clayton, adopted daughter of Mrs. Lubeck
Mrs. Marie Angela ten Bosch, widow, with J. Roderick and Adrian ten Bosch
hired man in back
Johnny Willilams, student on ground
John Schleiden with gun, student
Harold Clark, student

Sonoma Valley Historical Society

State of California required her to file a petition with the Superior Court of Sonoma County asking for permission to act as a "sole trader". This would enable Amelia to raise the necessary funds to pay for the new construction.[13]

In due time her petition was approved and Amelia became an equal with men to sell or obligate the property she already owned.

She began to hear requests from others in the valley to take in children as boarders. The widow Mrs. Marie Angela ten Bosch, from the Netherlands, asked Amelia to take in her three boys, John Roderick, Nicholas, and Adrian.

The story of Locust Grove is really the saga of Amelia Barbara Lubeck, a most extraordinary woman whose love for children and generous heart knew no limits.

By now the Locust Grove School, as Amelia's creation was known, was well established. She retained the title of principal and hired a headmaster. The first was Mr. Deering, who had been an Episcopal clergyman. The second was Mr. Badger, who soon earned the reputation that "he doesn't like boys."[14]

Among the teaching staff were Mrs. N. Davis who taught piano, and Miss Isabella Landsborough, one of Amelia's orphaned nieces from Australia, who taught painting and drawing. The principal gave lessons in modern languages, and Miss Florence Belnap had the English and Latin lower form classes. Miss Naomi Mitchell taught Spanish.

Included in the duties of the female teachers was to oversee the housekeeping chores of the students.

By 1880 the school was operating smoothly. Chi Kong, the Chinese cook, had a friend to help him, who stayed at the school until he returned to China in 1891.[15]

A hobo who came asking for a meal late one day not only received the meal, but was asked to stay and become the school handyman. He remained a number of years, as a valued member of the staff.

In spite of the many nonpaying children, Auntie Lubeck was able to charge reasonable rates for those who did pay. Their tuition for a 20-week term was $200 for those in the upper form (high school), $175 for the middle form, and $125 for the lower form. Music instruction was $20 extra and foreign language required an extra $10 per term.[16]

The school orchard produced several crops. The abundance of apples made the erection of an "apple house" necessary. Each year before they harvested the new crop, boys performed the duty of cleaning the house thoroughly. Scraps from the dining room fed the hogs. The chicken yard supplied the cook with eggs.

The school had enough peaches and pears to supply several neighbors. One neighbor who tilled the ground as needed was Julius Poppe. He was born in Berlin, Germany, and came to Sonoma in 1850. He had bought 1,500 acres of land, some of it marsh, from Mariano Vallejo, and succeeded in dairying. It was Poppe who planted the two rows of locust trees which still adorn either side of the school's driveway today.

Over the years Amelia Lubeck urged her parents to leave their home in Staten Island. They joined her in Sonoma and Amelia had a cottage built on the school grounds for them.

Life for the students was one joy after another. A favorite activity in good weather was taking a three-mile stroll after dinner into Sonoma. Sometimes the attraction was a church sermon, and at other times it was for the change of scenery. The walk home in the dark was remembered years later. "Walking home in the dark we'd sing the old favorites."[17]

Sonoma Creek, the old swimming hole, was a great place for all ages to enjoy. At one time several boys put in most of their spare hours building a boat so that they could fish up and down the creek.

The older boys organized a "brigade". Marching in formation became their goal. The one boy who came back from a visit home with a sword assumed the post of head of the brigade.[18]

Over the years since 1871, the Locust Grove Boarding School for Boys, as Auntie Lubeck advertised it, had been preparing boys for admission to the Episcopal colleges of St. Augustine at Benicia and St. Mathews Hall in San Mateo,[19] though there were also Roman Catholic students from Spanish-speaking homes enrolled in the school.

Their training did not prevent the students from playing pranks on their newly admitted fellows. One boy, Rafael Ramirez, whose family came from Costa Rica, was the target at the beginning of a term. He did not have a grasp of English yet, so while Auntie Lubeck was away, the older boys used the time to teach him a few words of greeting. The first teacher who welcomed Rafael heard him enthusiastically respond with "See the goddam dog."[20] Of course Miss Mitchell, the Spanish teacher, corrected him at once. Even he laughed at the trick the boys played on him. Diaz Martinez, from Culiacan, Mexico, also came to Locust Grove.

Located three miles from town on an often dusty or muddy dirt road, with little in Sonoma to interest them, the family of students at Locust Grove led an enjoyable life in the country, making use with what was at hand. Some of the boys asked for a duty which needed doing regularly. One such duty was granted to the boy who asked if he might work Maud and Beauty, who plowed or pulled the wagon or buggy, whichever needed moving.

John Roderick ten Bosch, one of the boys from the Netherlands, was dearly fond of horses and enjoyed the responsibility of their well being. His wish granted, one of his duties was to meet visitors to the school at the Schellville railroad station. He would hand-up the ladies into the buggy and drive off to home. Urging the team a little faster than necessary, he would turn the horses sharply at the end of the lane, skidding the wheels and side slipping up a slight cloud of gravel. He would dismount and reach to assist his passengers down. Then, very formally greet them with "Welcome to Locust Grove!"[21]

The ten Bosch brothers assisted at the school in many ways. John proposed starting a school newspaper. The idea probably struck him when he found an old press and type which had come to the school so long ago that no one could remember when. The boys had to set the type and run the press. They chose a format of four pages, each 4.5 by 6.25 inches. They charged $1 per year for a subscription.

To interest the public in the Schellville area, they included as much local news as they could. However every reference to the name Schellville is spelled "Shellville".

A favorite topic of the locals was the narrow gauge Sonoma Valley Railroad, whose terminal was in the Sonoma Plaza, but served the Schellville community at their own station. The boys picked up the criticism of the line, joining in with the locals. Their paper, the *Shellville Ray*, carried the following:

Locust Grove School

> The Sonoma Valley passenger train, because of fir-
> ing with wood of the greenest kind, which would
> not create a fire hot enough to keep up steam, was
> forced to stop no less than four times between
> Ignacio and Sonoma - some of the stops right in
> the midst of the tules.

Without a doubt the Locust Grove School provided many students with a stable and idyllic childhood, with abounding love from the founder and principal, Amelia Lubeck. References in the school newspaper reveal many activities shared by boys and girls, such as swimming, boating, tennis, and walking to town.

The overnight camping trips were strictly for boys however. An account of a very ambitious trip to Yosemite ran in the July 5, 1890 (vacation time) edition of the *Ray*.

> It was not our desire to go by prosaic steam, but in
> the more ideal way of coach and four! Our vehicle
> had a top with curtains.

They went through Oakland, Hayward and Livermore.

> At 6:30 we stopped at a ranch and found...a right
> jolly Teuton...who gives us cordial assent to our
> request for an abiding place for the night.

The next day the boys crossed the Altamont Pass by the old winding road. Here they speak of having to get out of their coach and help the horses by pushing. While they rode

The Shellville Ray.

IT SHINES TO BRIGHTEN THOSE WHO PAY.

VOL. IX. NO. 2.   SHELLVILLE, SEPT .23, 1893.   WHOLE NO. 147.

LOCUST GROVE SCHOOL.

Miss Madge Dowling spent last Saturday in San Francis-co.

Our teacher, Mr. T. N. Badger, has left us for the holidays.

The Misses Lindberg of San Francisco are visiting Locust Grove.

Mrs. S. A. Silvey was at the Grove to-day visiting her son Sydney.

Miss Ora Lawrence who left us recently for the State Normal School, writes cheerfully of life at the Garden City.

Miss Della Pauli and her brother Clayton are spending their vacation at their home at Terrace Hill near Sonoma.

Miss Mitchell left yesterday morning for Berkeley, San Francisco and other places, to visit friends before making her departure for Portland, Oregon.

Miss Landsborough who in company with her sister, Mrs. H. M. Whitely, has been visiting relatives in Florin, Sacramento county, returned to the Grove on Wednesday evening last. She came by way of San Francisco to see Irving and Terry.

Locust Grove welcomes one more boy to the ranks in the person of Edgar Lindsay. He arrived here last week in company with Dr. A. A. Waterhouse who made us a brief but pleasant visit.

The following scholars are spending the vacation in San Francisco: Lucille Kaiser, Stewart and Malcolm Elliott, Ralph Gwin, and Kenneth Mays. Cyrenius, Moltke has gone to Palo Alto.

Our old friend and school-mate Romaldo Diez Martinez and his cousin, Miss Tucker, were at the Grove on Sunday. Mr. Martinez will leave us in a few days for his home at Culiacan, Mexico. We wish him well.

The art exibition held in the schoolroom on Saturday evening, Sept. 9th., was a success in every way. The highest talent of Locust Grove was displayed and the work, which was all sold at auction brought handsome prices. The proceeds were turned over to the Locust Grove Lawn Tennis Club.

Sonoma Valley Historical Society
The Shellville Ray, Sept. 23, 1893

THE SHELLVILLE RAY,

PUBLISHED TWICE A MONTH AT
Shellville. Sonoma Co. Cal.

John R. tenBosch } Editor, publisher
and proprietor.

SUBSCRIPTION RATES:—50 cts. per
annum. Six months, 25 cts.

ADVERTISING RATES made known
on application.

Entered at the Shellville Post Office as
Second Class Mail Matter.

SHELLVILLE ... SEPT. 23, 1893.

THERE was a meeting of the California Amateur Press Association, in San Francisco, last Saturday. The editor of the RAY acknowledges an invitation to attend, and regrets being unable to make the trip.

LOCUST GROVE to-day is quiet. Vacation has begun and most of the students have gone to their homes to spend the week's holiday. The absence of so many faces is not unnoticed, and the merry voices that usually make the school grounds ring with shouts are not heard. There has been no mustering of the Boys' Brigade, no rallies at tennis; even the schoolroom must have missed the "detained boys," and the creek its fishermen. But it will last only for a week, and in good time on Monday morning, October 1st, we hope to see every boy in line, better prepared by a week's rest to continue his scholastic duties.

SHELLVILLE SIFTINGS.

Mr. Wm. Merriam spent Tuesday and Wednesday in Oakland.

Mrs. M. E. Cassebohm is visiting relatives at Oak Knoll, Napa County.

Miss Smythe, a former teacher of the San Luis School, is taking a special course in English at the Stanford University. There were 150 who took the entrance examination for this course but only thirty-six who passed—Miss Smythe being among the number.

"Toodles" has gone over to the silent majority. Toodles was the pet dog of Mr. Chas. Ohms of Embarcardero, and was a good natured little puppy Someone, though, had said he was "too cute to live," and the poor offended little fellow

Sonoma Valley Historical Society

The Shellville Ray, published twice a month at Shellville, Sonoma Co. Cal.

some of the way, they also walked many miles.

They made it to Yosemite and returned, proud of their accomplishment.

The vigilant staff of the *Shellville Ray* furnished more local news of particular note when they ran the following on February 18, 1891:

> The recent donation of $250 by Mrs. Robert Johnson of Buena Vista Park, for the benefit of improving the Sonoma Plaza, has been handed over to the Trustees of that city. A large force of men is now at work extending the plaza over the former site of the Sonoma Valley Railroad buildings; and the ground is being plowed up to admit the planting of shade trees at the very earliest possible date. Sonoma has a right to feel proud of her plaza. It was laid out by General Vallejo himself over fifty years ago. Of late years it has been much improved. Trees have been planted, walks repaired.

What the editor did not point out, because every citizen here knew it, was that the railroad had its station, round house, bunkers of wood for fuel and several auxiliary buildings on the plaza.

The editor ran some of these headings in almost every edition, "Sonoma Items", "Shellville Siftings", and "Locust Grove News".

Through the columns of the *Ray* we learn that Locust Grove had a tennis court, though probably it was a piece of ground run over by a handroller until smooth.

By September, 1892, Nicholas ten Bosch had given up the post of editor of the *Shellville Ray*. The new staff included C. Tilden, editor, and W. Strauch, business manager. Not content with the name of the paper, they called theirs the Weekly Sunbeam. It carried on in the same successful fashion as the *Ray*. The ten Bosch brothers later became leaders in the publishing and printing business in San Francisco.

If hiking back and forth to Sonoma wasn't enough walking, several of the boys longed for an overnight camping trip. Their plea to Auntie Lubeck for permission was granted. They settled on an ambitious undertaking, a 90-mile hike to see the Geysers.

They described their hike in the *Weekly Sunbeam* of September 10, 1893, the successor to the *Ray*. The students planned a walk which involved carrying their own baggage.

Full of enthusiasm and well rested, the boys hiked 22 miles to Santa Rosa on the first day of their experience. Since a circus and a balloon ascension were scheduled for the next day, the boys camped for two nights at the north end of the town.

The following morning they set out for Mark West Springs where the mill, operating by water power, intrigued them. They delayed and made camp near the mill.

The adventurers rose early, breakfasted and hiked through Calistoga, arriving at dusk at Kellogg. At the time,

Kellogg was the trailhead for the climb up Mt. St. Helena, and a lively place of amusement and a place to get a meal.

As on previous occasions, they asked farmers for permission to sleep in their fields. They cooked their own meals, continuing their journey through Knight's Valley and Alexander Valley. When they approached the road which climbed to the Geysers, they thoughtfully hid all their packs in the brush by the side of the road. They were glad they did, as the going was dusty and hot. On coming back, they recovered their packs, still intact.

Returning by way of Kellogg, they reported that there was a tavern with "parlor rifle shooting, bowling, croquet and lawn tennis." They estimated the hike at 17 miles from the Geysers to Kellogg. Continuing south, they retraced their steps through Calistoga, St. Helena, to Oakville. From there, they plodded their way up the Oakville Grade and down to Glen Ellen. They went to the house of one of the boys' uncle. After bathing and eating a hot meal, they slept.

In 1892 a dear friend of Auntie Lubeck died. She was the neighbor Amelia Clayton. She left three girls, Della, May, and Amy, the youngest. To them Auntie Lubeck became "Grandma". She formally adopted them.

As the Clayton children grew, they were given responsibilities and worked with Bella Landsborough, a rock of cheerful competence and a talented artist who had been

Sonoma Valley Historical Society, Mrs. Robert Kiser collection

Locust Grove School, dormitory, dining room and kitchen. Built in the 1870s, it still stands in 1997

given more of the responsibilities of both managing the school and seeing to the housekeeping.

The students tended the farm animals, gathered vegetables, and picked fruit. They prepared the peaches, pears, apples, plums, and cherries for jams and jellies. They tended rents in knickers, holes in socks, scrubbed necks and ears, made beds, turned mattresses, emptied slop pails, ripped up old and tacked down new "matting" (discarding the old newspapers and laying down fresh underneath). They went to classes too, and even had time for music lessons.[22]

The boys' greatest joy was outside the classroom when they had the run of a working farm with a hayloft, horses, cows, geese, chickens, rabbits, cats and dogs. There were berry patches, swarming bees, bird nests, squirrels, frogs, snakes, a creek for swimming and fishing, and trees for climbing and swinging.

The discipline imposed was one of daily routine, with regular class hours, hearty meals, evening prayers, nightly scrubs, and kissing "Auntie" good night.

For more formal fun there was horseshoe pitching, croquet and tennis. And inside in the evening there was singing together while Ethel Pauli played the little organ in the parlor. Games were checkers and "Beast, Bird, or Fish."

Older boys left and younger ones came, but many returned years later to visit Auntie Lubeck and the school of their youth.

The social life included the annual May picnic. Huge lunch baskets were packed. A farm wagon loaded with children and adults was pulled by two horses for the ten or twelve miles to a favorite picnic spot in Glen Ellen.[23]

There came a time when Charles W. Lubeck found that no one would hire him for their crew. He turned back to his wife and appealed to her for a place to stay. With forgiveness in her heart she made a place for him on the school grounds. She took him in even though over the years he spent most of his time wandering through the orchard, often just sitting on the ground with his back to a tree trunk. The students saw the former sea captain at meal times but he was seldom seen elsewhere.

Charles W. Lubeck died on March 14, 1893 at the age of 79. The Coroner listed the cause of death as a brain concussion. He was buried at the Mountain View Cemetery in Sonoma.[24]

The number of pupils increased over the years and finally in 1897 Mrs. Lubeck brought in graduates from the University of California at Berkeley to teach at the school. Among those were Frank Argell, Allen Smith, and Elmer Rowell.[25]

Unified by the loving heart of Mrs. Lubeck, Locust Grove was a lively family in 1900, with about twenty students. The three teachers lived on the property in a small building in the apple orchard called the Cottage.

Beside the teachers, the staff which helped run the school included the stalwart Bella Landsborough and the capable and beautiful Pauli girls, the Chinese cooks Hing and Chang, and the handyman John Wilson. He was called Uncle Jack and had been captain of a boat that plied the sloughs and bay to San Francisco. He made his headquarters at Locust Grove. Meals were served at a large family dining table. Mrs. Lubeck was at the head, and a prayer was offered before all meals.[26]

For sixteen years after her husband's death, Mrs. Lubeck continued her organization. The earthquake of 1906 shook the frame buildings but did no damage.

Lubeck ran a successful boarding school, from the arrival of her orphaned nieces and nephews in 1869, until her death in 1909 at the age of 78. Locust Grove School closed at that time.

Many former students wrote letters which were kept in a trunk in the old two-story school building. One wrote

> Mrs. Lubeck's success lay in the sincere simplicity of her nature. She met the challenge of previous husbands with faith and courage and became in fact a pillar of strength for others less valiant.[27]

Amelia "Auntie" Lubeck
Sonoma Valley Historical Society

Another wrote

The light this noble little pioneer woman kindled should never be allowed to dim but that its radiance should illumine and irradiate the lives and minds and souls of children. This world is a better world for having Amelia Lubeck on it.[28]

Credits

Let no one ever think this work could be done alone. I am genuinely grateful for the generous assistance of several people who aided me and became my friends.

First of all, my son Roger, who researched and wrote the chapter on Saint Mary's Hall, has always been my dearest critic and gives me the best guidance any parent may hope for.

Secondly, Mrs. Robert Kiser, a long time Sonoma resident in whose protective custody the Peterson papers are resting. She rescued them from firemen who threw out a partially burned trunk and intended to take it to the garbage dump. Mrs. Kiser kindly made these valuable pieces of history available to me.

I must thank the departed Mrs. Elmer Peterson, who saved and collected anything pertaining to the Locust Grove Boarding School for Boys. She saved letters from everyone who wrote inquiring about the school and made a list over the years of the alumni and relatives of former students who came to visit. They recalled hearing about or being involved in many happy experiences at the school. Mrs. Peterson's list is a very long one.

Mr. Stefan Buffy, manager of the Sonoma Branch of the County Library system found the only (known to us) 16-

page catalog for the 1861 school year of the Cumberland Presbyterian College. It revealed many secrets hidden for a century and a half. He went out of his way to assist us with other sources.

Diane Smith, a long-time member of the Sonoma Valley Historical Society, discovered more than fifty copies of the *Shellville Ray* and the *Weekly Sunbeam*. The boys who wrote for those newspapers were recording intimate history which lasted for more than a century. Thanks go to Diane for calling them to my attention.

Notes

[1] Peterson Collection, Mrs. Robert Kiser, Sonoma

[2] Jack Tracy, *Sausalito, Moments In Time*, Sausalito: Windgate Press, 1983.

[3] Jack Mason and Helen Van Cleave, *Early Marin*, Inverness, CA: North Shore Books, 1976.

[4] ibid.

[5] ibid.

[6] Sonoma County Records, Book of Deeds "E", pages 101, 143, 151

[7] C.A. Menefee, *Sonoma County Biographies*, Napa City 1878

[8] Sonoma County Records, Book of Deeds "K", page 5: "Thomas O. Larkin of the City of San Francisco am bound to Lubeck & Co. of the City of San Francisco…on September 25, 1852…for $4,000 for which Thos. O. Larkin is bound to deliver 192.75 acres."

[9] Menefee, op. cit.

[10] Barbara Annette Smith, "Locust Grove School", typewritten manuscript [n.d.], Robert Parmelee collection.

[11] Peterson collection

[12] Meta Stofen, "Locust Grove School" in *Saga of Sonoma*, Sonoma: The Sonoma Valley Historical Society, 1976, p.18.

[13] Peterson collection

[14] ibid.

[15] *Shellville Ray*

[16] Peterson collection

[17] ibid.

[18] ibid.

[19] ibid.

[20] ibid.

[21] *Shellville Ray*

[22] Smith, op. cit.

[23] ibid.

[24] Sonoma County Recorder's Office

[25] ibid.

[26] Smith, op. cit.

[27] Peterson collection

[28] ibid.

The Scows of Sonoma Creek

Waterways were the principal transportation routes in early California. Passengers and freight travelled around San Francisco Bay and up the great rivers of the Sacramento and the San Joaquin. Even the tributaries which drain into the bay, such as the Petaluma and Napa rivers and Sonoma Creek, were crucial to the development of towns and an agricultural economy.

At first, fishing boats could be used to carry small consignments. But before long, steamers and sailboats plied any creek or slough which would accommodate their size.

It was during the American period, after 1846, that the narrow Sonoma Creek became an important route that connected the Sonoma Valley with the goods and services available in San Francisco.

The earliest recorded transportation system on Sonoma Creek points to the year 1847, three years before California

Sonoma Valley Historical Society, Groskopf collection

This scow schooner is filled with 250-300 lb. five wire bales and will sail to China Basin, San Francisco. Note the furled jib.

became a state. The Russian-built paddle wheel steamer, the 37-foot *Sitka* arrived in San Francisco Bay. It began regular passenger service between San Francisco and Sonoma, which was the only well organized town north of the Golden Gate.

A competitor, the sloop *Stockton*, began the same service in November. Captain Briggs of the *Stockton* advertised his vessel as a "fast sailor". It probably was fast when it departed Sonoma with a northwest breeze behind it and the ebb tide boosting him on his way. But when he had to buck the wind and river current, the ship was anything but fast.

When these two vessels made their trips, they accommodated mainly passengers and some freight. However, surely some of Agoston Haraszrthy's wine went on board to help satisfy the San Francisco restaurant owners.

In those early days, noisy Mexican oxcarts bounced over rough roads, taking people and cargo from the town plaza in Sonoma to the Embarcadero landing just three miles south of town. There they boarded a steamer which would take them to San Francisco. By 1849 people could ride from town in a little more comfort in a "lumbering old passenger coach".[1]

A cluster of a few houses and barns at the Embarcadero became known as St. Louis or San Luis. In 1851 Englishman Frank Marryat wrote this description of the village.

Schools and Scows in Early Sonoma

> Here are three houses; opposite the town some fish-
> ing boats lay at anchor, and in one of these I bar-
> gained for a passage to San Francisco, in company
> with eight live bullocks, that were now lying on
> the strand, bound neck and heels together, moan-
> ing piteously, as if impatient to get to the butcher's
> and have it all over. With the exception of the own-
> ers of the three houses, the population of San Luis
> was a particularly floating one, being represented
> for the most part by crews of the fishing smacks,
> of which there were at times a great number in port.

A letter in the files of the Sonoma Valley Historical Society describes the condition in the late 1850s, suggesting that
better passenger service was available through Benicia.[2]

> It was a long trip to Benicia in those days. No real
> roads and far distances (from Los Guilicos). For
> some years that was the way to San Francisco, driv-
> ing to Benicia and taking a boat to the city. Later,
> they went to the Embarcadero, or to Petaluma,
> which was now becoming a thriving town. In all
> cases, it was a matter of struggling through deep
> mud and chuck holes in winter and through smoth-
> ering dust in the summer. It was a common sight
> to see heavy clumsy wagons drawn by oxen, six
> and eight of them drawing heavy loads.

The growing population of Sonoma Valley needed better passenger service. In 1862, an advertisement appeared
in the Santa Rosa Democrat, indicating the first regular passenger service.

> Steamer *Princess* will leave Sonoma on Monday,
> Wednesday, & Friday @ 10 a.m. for San Francisco

Such teams of sixteen to twenty horses, used by well-to-do farmers and farm contractors, were beyond the means of the average farmer.

Author's collection

and will return every Tuesday, Thursday and Saturday at 11 a.m. Stages depart for Santa Rosa,
Healdsburg same day.

Without good roads for teams of horses or oxen, farmers depended on water transportation to sell their produce and to buy supplies. Bay scows served the needs of farmers and many businesses for almost sixty-five years.

The flat bottom bay scow or hay scow was an ideal vehicle to carry cargo around the bay region. It had a level deck, clear of protuberances. It could carry long lengths of lumber and pipe, barrels of wine, and lug boxes of fruit. It also delivered farm produce and enormous loads of bales of hay, sacks of grain, dressed stone for buildings and paving stones for San Francisco streets.

Looking down from overhead on the open deck of the scow, one would see the bowsprit protruding from the bow and masts or mast rising from the deck, with only two hatches marring the entire deck space. The first hatch would be over the centerboard and it would lie flush with the deck. The other would be the covered scuttle. It would be very near the stern, an opening about three feet square, leading down to the cooking and bunk area. Back of the scuttle was the cockpit and wheel and finally the stern rail.

The steering arrangements were very inge-
nious and rather spectacular. The tiller ropes

led from the steering wheel drum via blocks and fairleads to the rudder and back aboard to a cleat. When a high deck load of hay was being carried, naturally the helmsmen's view was obscured. To get around this problem, the tiller ropes were cast off and the wheel and drum unshipped from the harp. One arrangement had a six by six timber of the appropriate height erected with a small platform on top, while another used two 2 x 6s. The wheel was transferred to the platform and the tiller ropes (which were long enough) set taught. The helmsman now could look over the top of the deck load. In order to get to his perch, a regular wooden rung ladder was lashed to the post and he climbed to his station.[3]

The design had a square, blunt bow, which was slightly narrower than the stern. The sides from overhead were slightly bowed. The maximum beam width would be a little forward of midship.[4]

The rig was a moderate one, but it had two very practical characteristics. Both the foresail (on the schooner) and gaff rigged main had three rows of reef points and the mainmast was a disproportionately tall topmast. The reef points were used for raising the boom over the hay load which was five or seven tiers high.[5]

The reef points also made it possible to raise the booms so that they would clear the levees and brush along the banks in the delta country.[6] The centerboard was heavy, sometimes over a ton in weight.

The scows always towed a 10- to 12-foot lap straked din-
ghy. It was occasionally needed to tow the scow when she
was becalmed, especially near a landing.

From underneath, the bottom consisted of 3" by 12" bottom planks fastened 'thwartship. While it has long been
customary for longitudinal planks on "V"-shaped hulls, it
would never do to have that shape of hull on a scowl. Often
the scows would run head onto a bank in a creek, lay out a
sturdy plank on shore, and then load cargo by hand or by
handtruck. Lug boxes of fruit and sacks of grain would be
handtrucked onto the scow's deck. The flat bottom hull
would help maintain a level deck.

The scow had been in use in New England since colonial
times. On the Pacific Coast, a Santa Cruz boat builder completed a boat he named *Bloody Box* in 1848.[7] The name de-
picted the shape of the craft.

The design was a simple one which was economical to
operate. It took only one man to sail the sloop and two to
man the schooner.

While registration of vessels equipped with engines gen-
erally has been observed, the same has not been the case
with sail boats built by individuals. Most scows were built
in shipyards and registered. An unknown number were constructed by sea going carpenters who did not register their
work. For those vessels registered, a "Master Carpenter's

Certificate" was issued by the Collector of Customs, giving the dimensions and the name of the builder.

Most scows slid down the ways at Hunters Point in San Francisco.[8] Both Anderson & Christofani and Emil Munder operated there. Matthew Turner built more at his Benicia yard. Scows were cheap to build.

People gave scows several names. One writer said "a hay scow has a hermaphrodite appearance as if she is a love child, crossbred from a landing craft and a river barge."[9]

A sloop-rigged scow crew consisted of the captain who was the owner, and a mate who served as cook and sailor and who helped load and unload cargo. On a schooner one more man joined the crew. Hired hands stayed with the ship only if they could cook.

Sleeping quarters were inside at the stern where there was room for a man to lay on his blankets, one on each side of the hull with very little headroom. They were wedged in between the main deck and the beams above the bottom. The galley fit in a box-like house aft on the deck.

The first sailing scow to make Sonoma Creek its home port must have been the sloop *Mariese* (Mary S). William Green, her owner, arrived in California in 1847. A soldier in Stevenson's New York Volunteers, he came to Sonoma in early April when Company "C" arrived and with his comrades took up residence in the Barracks.[10]

Captain Green's *Mariese* was small and in use during the 1850s and the early 1860s. He often sailed her with a load of hay bound for the San Francisco hay wharf on the south side of the China Basin Channel.[11]

With one crewman Green would load the hay as high as 14 feet with bales weighing 250-300 pounds. It usually took them one day to load, another day to make the China Basin Channel, and a third day to unload.[12]

With the *Mariese* empty, Green would sail along the waterfront to Meiggs Wharf. There he would buy a load of lumber for himself and with his crewman load every stick of wood by hand.

He would wait for the outgoing tide to ebb before setting out on the return to Sonoma Creek. Then he would set sail on the incoming tide to boost him northward so that he could pass over the bar at Sonoma Creek at high water.

Captain Green became frustrated with the small loads the *Mariese* carried, and ultimately sold her in order to buy two scow schooners. The *Hamlet*, the smaller of the two, and the *Marguerite*, were both built in San Francisco. After a few years he sold the *Marguerite*, but the *Hamlet* sailed for her owner many years.

The Captain correctly estimated he could make more money selling lumber from a yard he acquired in St. Louis, across the road from the Embarcadero. A store supplied those in the neighborhood with the necessities. Vollmer's two-story hotel supplied respite to travelers and workmen when needed, and a livery stable completed the businesses there.

Green's home and several others helped occupy St. Louis. Numerous warehouses lined the banks of the creek opposite the town.

By 1863 Captain Green was not sailing, but spent all his time selling lumber.

Where Green left off, the Stofen brothers, Peter and J.J. Stofen, took over. They came to Sonoma in 1862 and bought some of the best farm land when they acquired almost 200 acres along the east side of Sonoma Creek running south from St. Louis.[13] Stofen Landing was the first below the Embarcadero. The brothers built a large warehouse for storage of crops awaiting sale and shipment.

By this time Sonoma had meat and game to ship to San Francisco. Farmers had pumpkins, beets, turnips, and an abundance of onions and peas to ship. In good time the Stofens had hundreds of lug boxes of peaches for the San Francisco market.

The brothers sailed the *Alice Stofen*, a sloop-rigged scow of only 18 tons displacement, built in San Francisco.[14] With shipping capacity growing in part due to demand for wine and wine grapes, as well as paving and building stones, the

The Alice Stofen as she appeared as a whaler. Note the harpoon gun on the foredeck.

San Francisco Maritime National Historical Park

brothers had the 53-foot *J.J. Stofen* built in Charles G. White's yard in San Francisco. She had a beam of 21 feet and a draft of only 4.5 feet. Her displacement was rated at 32.35 tons.

The Stofens also sailed the *Gazelle*. This sloop-rigged scow was only 36 feet long with a draft of 4.2 feet. She was fast and her speed attracted future buyers such as Captain Hauto and later Captain Green once more.

The *Mary Francis* was another "square toed" scow to sail out of Sonoma Creek. No record of her ownership has been located.

With a cargo of cheese in boxes, barrels of wine or maybe lug boxes of fresh fruit from Sonoma orchards, scows delivered their cargoes to docks around San Francisco Bay.

Some deliveries were to the docks along the Oakland Estuary. When returning, since they were facing the prevailing afternoon brisk wind, captains often chose to pay steam tug captains $1.50 for a tow out of the estuary to Goat Island.

From early on, scows departing from the Embarcadero near Sonoma were loaded with firewood destined for the "wood and coal wharf" in San Francisco. Owners of the many small coal and wood yards which dotted each neighborhood throughout San Francisco carted their supply from this wharf.

One steamer which plied Sonoma Creek in the 1850s was

the *Georgina*. Captain Peter Justi of Glen Ellen ordered her built and ran her from Sonoma to San Francisco making three round trips each week. Passenger fare was $20 each way.

Apparently in the 1860s Petaluma offered more revenue than Sonoma, and the *Georgina* was more often found on that route rather than on Sonoma Creek. One day in 1865, at the Petaluma landing the *Georgina* boiler exploded. Five people died in the accident, including Captain Robinson. Several more were seriously wounded, including passengers George Frank, G. Bush, and Valentine Iken, and fireman John Flood. Eight or ten persons were missing after the accident, including Captain Thompson. Captain Hoyt, U.S. Inspector of Hulls and Steamboats, said for the last three trips there had been no engineer on the steamer, one of the fireman acting in that capacity.[15]

The demand for paving stones first came from San Francisco. The Sonoma quarries on Schocken Hill provided the principal supply. It furnished both granite and basalt rock. The quarry on the east side of First Street West is still evident. Sonoma still abounds in basalt. Rock came from Trinity Road and from behind General Vallejo's home. Italian stone cutters were available in Sonoma from early days. When the first Sebastiani arrived in the area, he went to work as a stone cutter for $1 per day. He later received $1.50 for working a 12-hour day.

Scows

The demand from San Francisco at first was for building blocks. Like those used in constructing the old city hall in Sonoma, some churches in San Francisco were built with Sonoma stone. The San Francisco Embarcadero, originally East Street, had a seawall made with the same material.

San Jose was a second market for dressed stone. Scow captains enjoyed the sail south to Alviso, as they could stay on the starboard tack all the way.

Workmen used wheelbarrows when either loading or unloading bricks or dressed stone. Scow schooners carried them on deck only 3.5 to four feet high because of their weight.

One Sonoma quarryman, H.C. Manuel, shipped one order for 150,000 dressed stones to Stockton.[16] Later he received another order for 100,000 blocks.

A San Francisco cable car company also bought 100,000 blocks in a single order. They used the blocks to fit between the tracks and the cable slot.

The Sonoma scow fleet simply could not deliver very many of the blocks shipped. Steam tugs towed barges loaded at the Embarcadero up the San Joaquin River with most of the Stockton orders. And later the railroad took some on flat cars.

Asphalt, the sludge in an oil refinery, wasn't available in northern California until the first refinery began operation at Alameda Point in the late 1880s.[17] The supply came slowly in the first decade of operation and the City of San Francisco monopolized the supply.

When the wine grapes were picked and readied for shipment, a big part of the harvest was shipped to Italians in San Francisco who made their own wine. The grapes went in lug boxes on scows to a buyer's basement where the vats were located. Meiggs Wharf and Fishermans Wharf were handy for the North Beach customers to cart their grapes home by horse and buggy.

Landings were created wherever farmers had substantial crops to ship. Many landings had a platform and a warehouse. Most warehouses were large to accommodate sacked grain or five-wire bales of hay.[18]

Coming up the Sonoma Creek from San Pablo Bay, the first landing was Essex, and then Norfolk. The Sonoma Valley Railroad referred to this location as Wingo, and a bridge crossed the creek at this point. A lift span there was operated by hand. A chain ran over a series of sprockets so that it took little effort to lift the span. The bridge was decked over with solid planking so that people could ride their horses over the bridge. One resident of the area allowed his young boy to drive his horse and carriage over the bridge to school.[19] However, the bridge tender always led the horse by its bridal. The railroad company had constructed a house

Sonoma Valley Historical Society, Groskopf collection

Eight wagons have brought assorted commodities consigned to San Francisco to the sailing scow schooner at the Sonoma Embarcadero for the tender adjacent to the bridge so that he would be available at all times.

Upstream from Norfolk was Poppes Landing, then Stofen Landing, and the last, Sonoma Embarcadero and St. Louis.

The constant hard work of lifting bales and barrels eventually took its toll on several of the Sonoma Creek scow owners. They agreed there was a more acceptable way to live. They formed a partnership and ordered a 109-foot stern wheel steamer to be built. Captain William Green and the Stofen brothers each came in for a one-quarter interest. Peter Hauto and Mary O. Faucett each subscribed for a one-eighth share.[20]

They named the steamer *Sonoma*. She slid down the ways in San Francisco on September 30, 1874. Even though she was of 179 tons displacement, she drew only five feet of water.

She ran for a few years between Petaluma and San Francisco. She was on that run because her owners had spent more money than the traffic from Sonoma could warrant.

The California Transportation Co. of Stockton bought her and put her on an overnight run from Stockton to San Francisco.

First, her new owners lengthened the *Sonoma* from 109 feet to 135 feet.[21] This increased her displacement from 179

Sonoma Valley Historical Society

Rear paddle wheel steamer Sonoma, 109 feet long, was launched in 1874. She is departing, going down Sonoma Creek.

to 250 tons. Because the *Sonoma* was now catering to the overnight traveler, with berths and meals, she carried a crew of fourteen.

The *Sonoma* appeared last in the 1923 publication "Merchant Steam Vessels of the United States". She dropped out of its pages in 1924, fifty years after she made her debut on the waters of San Francisco Bay.

When the tide flowed on the incoming or ebb, the current pushed the water up to six miles per hour past the San Francisco waterfront piers.

Scow captains depended only on wind power, unless they were among the few to have an engine to drive them, to bring them to the dock.

When approaching a pier in a strong current, the scow captain made ready the 400-500 feet of mooring line carried on board.[22] Usually the mate pulled in the painter of the trailing skiff. When he had it alongside, he lowered himself into it while the captain tossed him one end of the mooring line. He would quickly grab an oar and scull vigorously for a receding wharf pile. He made fast to it and quickly rowed as hard as he could back to his scow. There he climbed on board and ran forward to make fast his end of the line to a bitt in the bow. Slowly, with the aid of a hand winch forward, the scow rounded and warped to the pier.

The Master Mariners Association held its July 4th regatta

Sonoma Valley Historical Society

The S.S. Sonoma after workers spliced a 26-foot section between the bow and superstructure area.

as usual in 1869. This annual event is still staged on San Francisco Bay. The entrants gathered like flies around the starting line, usually off the end of the Market or Howard Street wharves. Boats of various sizes and classes each raced in a division of their own. While it looked to spectators like a free for all, nevertheless the judges made their decisions according to predetermined rules. The starting time of each vessel was recorded as it crossed the line. Stake boats were anchored off Hunters Point, thence to another off the Oakland bar and finally to the last stake boat off Fort Point and then back to Meiggs Wharf or the seawall. Such a course covered about 22 miles.

In the 1869 regatta the 36-foot *Gazelle* won in the sloop division, beating even much larger boats. In 1871 the *Gazelle* again beat every boat in her class. In 1872 and 1873 Captain Green came out of retirement and nailed down the scow's reputation.

In 1873 the regatta committee gave her permanent possession of the "Champions" banner. Rules forbade her entering the races after her triple honors, but she sailed anyway in 1874 and swept the fleet. As if to deign the honors he had just won, instead of attending the Grand Ball, Captain Green and the *Gazelle* sailed away headed for home at Norfolk. However, as if he was reticent about the award, the Captain returned the white silk and red-trimmed Cham-

National Maritime Museum

The 36-foot champion scow sloop Gazelle, empty of cargo, nears the entrance to Sonoma Creek.

pion banner to the committee. Later it found a home in the National Maritime Museum in San Francisco where it can be seen today.

A newspaper article described the variety of freight, not only hay, which came out of Sonoma. From the *Sonoma Index-Tribune* of September 21, 1878:

> The sloop *Gazelle*, owned by the genial Captain Hauto, plying between Embarcadero and San Francisco, is doing a heavy freight business. The principal consignments to the metropolis at present consist of wine and table grapes. On her return trips large quantities of lumber and miscellaneous merchandise are stored in her capacious hold.

The Sonoma Valley Railroad began operations in 1879. The narrow gauge line did siphon off a small portion of the revenue that had been going to the scows. But it was not long before an entirely new shipper appeared on the scene.

More than 10,000 acres of swamp lay between what is today State Route 37 and the Sonoma to Napa highway. It was worthless to all but a former U.S. Senator from Nevada. John P. Jones (1873-1903) made a substantial fortune in the Comstock Lode silver discovery at Virginia City, Nevada.[23]

With not only money but also foresight, Senator Jones created Pacific Reclamation Co., a corporation. He ordered two clam shell dredgers built and delivered to San Pablo Bay. Put to work, the dredgers widened and deepened

Robert Parmelee Collection

This Sonoma Valley Railroad narrow gauge train ran from Sonoma to Ignacio about 1880

Sonoma Valley Historical Society, Groskopf colloection

The ticket office and waiting room of the Wingo station on Sonoma Creek, formerly Norfolk. This was a busy place with hunters in duck season.

Sonoma Valley Historical Society, Groskopf collection

Bridge tender Louis Semino on the Wingo bridge, 1902-1935. The original bridge was built in 1879 by the Sonoma Valley Railroad, and was replaced in 1921 by the present bridge. It is subject to opening, and it does so on average less than twice a year.

Sonoma Creek and then turned east toward the swamps. Here they made channels as they built levees around what became six islands.

In an interlocking ownership, when the Pacific Reclamation work was finished, the land that now drained through headgates was ready for breaking up the peat. It was plowed and prepared for planting oats for hay. Producers Hay Co. of San Francisco took over. They built self sufficient camps for workers on each of the six islands. Each provided kitchens and sleeping quarters for the workers.[24]

Next they constructed large warehouses where they could store, out of inclement weather, and ship to San Francisco whenever the price was attractive. Being the cheapest form of transportation, scows carried all of Producers Hay crops to the terminal at China Basin in San Francisco.

Captain Peter Hauto was sailing his scow schooner, the 58.5 foot long *Four Sisters*.[25] She was built in Matthew Turner's yard in Benicia. She was equipped with an engine. Hauto catered to the fruit shipping businesses. The *Four Sisters* was the last of the scow schooners to serve Sonoma Valley.

With Contra Costa County growing as much tonnage of fresh fruit as any Bay Area county, scows seeking fruit shipments gravitated to the small creeks of the southern shore of the San Joaquin River. From Antioch to Brentwood and

Sonoma Valley Historical Society, Groskopf collection

The clam shell dredger Nevada, the first of two operated by the Pacific Reclamation Co. Its boom is 90 feet long.

Sonoma Valley Historical Society, Groskopf collection
*This scow schooner is under power with all sails furled as it heads up
Sonoma Creek to one of the Producers Hay Co. six camps.*

Byron, hundreds of acres yielded big crops of peaches, pears and apricots.

Loaded in lug boxes, the fruit was stacked higher than the navigator's head. However, standing on the top rung of his tall ladder he could see his way.

One day in the 1890s the *Four Sisters* was sailing downstream in the San Joaquin River. She was loaded with all the grain she could carry. About opposite Antioch the four man crew was surprised by water sloshing along the deck and creeping into the bottom layer of sacks. In probably less than a minute, the cry rang out, "Jump for it!"

Apparently the bottom planks had separated, water filled the hold and the *Four Sisters* went under with all her load. The four men swam for shore and survived.

After Captain Hauto lost his schooner, he turned to Captain Green and bought the *Gazelle*. Soon after he made the purchase a San Francisco newspaper told of an experience that happened to Hauto and his mate. The story appeared on July 18, 1890.

> Captain Hauto and John Wilson, first mate of the sloop Gazelle, are the heroes of the day. Late last evening as they were discharging their cargo, a splash was heard, and almost immediately a cry burst out "Help! Help!" rang out in the cool night air. A rush for the sloop's boat was made, and while the painter was cast off by the captain, Wilson made ready with the oars. A moment later and the

National Maritime Museum

Scow schooner Four Sisters in Sonoma Creek loaded with fruit and vegetables.

Sonoma Valley Historical Society

This gasoline powered scow carried as much hay as five sailing scow schooners. The Reginia S. was 68 feet long and slid down the ways in 1893. Note the gangplank to handtruck bales on board.

skiff was flying across the water to rescue the unknown man, who when reached, was in an unconscious condition. Mr. Wilson grabbed him just as he was going down for the last time, and hauled him in over the stern, after which he was taken on board the nearest boat and brought back to consciousness.

From Sonoma Creek, the Producers Hay Co. kept the home based scows busy. But the veteran sailing scows gradually became outdated and the owners found it difficult to keep up with the demand. An opportunity for larger and faster vessels was evident.

In 1893 several ship owners built large motorized scows to haul hay initially just for Producers Hay Co.

The first, the *Regina S.*, 68 feet long, was built to carry 35 tons. Three similar craft followed her, the *Ondine*, *Mary* and *McKenna*. All four were equipped with gasoline engines. They each carried five times as much hay as a schooner.

At the turn of the century, the *J.J. Stofen* was in the hands of Captain Milson. Stranger tales than his are seldom heard in scow circles. His unusual and near fatal experience took place during the first week of September, 1900. When the captain tied up at the McNear wharf at the foot of Western Avenue in Petaluma he had this story to tell.

The *Stofen* was skimming over the bay with every sail set. The wind churned the shallow water as we approached San Pablo Bay, and I told the mate to take in sail. The mate was obeying the order and standing with a line in his hand when the boom of the forward sail swung around, struck him a terrific blow in the back and literally pitched him into the bay. The blow forced him clear of the schooner's side.

The mate was stunned and helpless. The cold water brought him partially to. Involuntarily he closed his hand on the rope when he was hurled overboard and he continued his hold all the time he was partially unconscious.

I was helpless in the mate's plight. The big spread of the sail and the wind made the schooner behave like an unbroken colt. I clung to the wheel.

When the mate regained consciousness he took a half turn around his wrist with the rope and for nine miles the schooner towed him.

The small boat astern swung almost within his reach a number of times but never came within his reach. Finally it did swing his way and he caught it. He somehow managed to climb in. He rode in the small boat until we reached the mouth of the Petaluma River when I lowered sail and got the mate aboard.

Ashore at last, the mate seemed ashamed of his adventure and refused to relate any particulars.[26]

Much later, in August 1906, John F. Scheller took delivery of the launch *Sonoma Valley*. She was powered by gas according to the Master Carpenter's Certificate dated July 9, 1906. She was 54 feet long and built of wood, with a beam of 18' 6". She drew 4' 7" of water. August K. Schultze built her in Fairhaven, California and she homeported in San Francisco. There is very little record of her travels, only "The *Sonoma Valley* came up Schell Slough."

One day in early April, 1907, Captain Hauto didn't ap-

Robert Parmelee collection

The Sonoma Valley, *built in 1906, was powered by a gasoline engine. Note the Wingo Bridge superstructure in the background.*

pear on time at his house at Essex Landing. The night before his boat had grounded about one mile below his home. The mate, John Wilson, and the balance of the crew had left the captain to walk home.

The following morning Wilson went back to look for his friend. He found Hauto's hat and pipe out on deck. He also found blood stains on an iron bar which "projected from the sides." The search ended when he discovered Hauto's body partially wedged under the hull.[27]

The coroner's inquest stated that Captain Hauto died from accidental trauma to the head. Captain Hauto was laid to rest at Mountain Cemetery in Sonoma.

Sailing scows continued to survive on San Francisco Bay, furnishing low cost, if somewhat slow, freight hauling of merchandise. They moved freight expeditiously on regardless of weather condition. They could work on foggy days, as well as on calm and rainy days. Estimates made in 1900 claimed 300 scows remained in the trade. While several survived, their usefulness disappeared by 1915.

The Stofen brothers left the scow life in diverse ways. J.J. Stofen hired out to the U.S. Government. He became master of the *General McDowell*, which served the federal interest in San Francisco Bay and river waters. Peter Stofen retired to his home on Broadway Avenue in Sonoma, having sold the *Alice Stofen* to a whaling operator. She continued to have a useful and long life, from 1866 to 1915.

Those who watched scows from the deck of a ferryboat and others who saw the crews loading or unloading have questioned why someone would work so hard day after day.

Those spectators who looked on as a scow captain made the decisions as to which freight went on his boat first and which was the lightest to go on top hardly envied him.

To see the skipper decide which part of the load should go midship and which, the lighter, should be stowed near the bow and which to stack on the stern one might wonder at his skill. Also, he would place crates or sacks evenly so as to keep the craft level.

After loading, the captain cast off the lines and began to navigate down the twists and turns of Sonoma Creek. The jib filled and with a keen eye he kept his craft in the deepest course of the channel.

Once out on San Pablo Bay, he set his sail on the starboard tack, with the boom out to port. Meanwhile he had time to watch the shore birds flying and the gulls diving for a meal.

The captain might light his pipe and feel the tranquility, the stretch of pure delight only a seaman knows. Work at a desk in an office? Clerk in a store? Never. He had the proud exultation of one who sailed and was his own master.

Sonoma Valley Historical Society, Groskopf collection

This Producer Hay Co. White truck with solid rubber tires, about1914, is in front of the company warehouse at 176 Townsend St., San Francisco.

Credits

Diane Smith, keeper of the archives at the Sonoma Valley Historical Society Museum, deserves far more recognition than I can give, for her aid in supplying me with the scarce material I needed to write these pages.

Mary Rede, reference librarian at the Sonoma branch of the county library system, somehow discovered several publications now out of print, and retrieved them for me. They provided ideas used in writing this manuscript.

Every reader should know that most of the best photographs in this work came from the family album collections of Mr. And Mrs. Charles Groskopf of Sonoma. I salute them for their willingness to allow me to copy whatever I wished.

Robert Parmelee must have the most extensive collection of historical material, including maps, original manuscripts, early printed books and a generous attitude which gave me access to all of it. He directed me to several sources from which I gleaned information which made this work come alive. He is also the author of *Pioneer Sonoma*.

Notes

[1] Eliza Donner Houghton, *The expedition of the Donner party and its tragic fate*. Los Angeles: Grafton Publishing Corp., 1920.

[2] Marion Shaw Sneyd-Kynnersley, "Stories I have heard of Los Guilicos", typwritten manuscript, Sonoma Valley Historical Society.

[3] Richard Boss, *Nautical Research Journal*, National Maritime Museum, 1984, p.113.

[4] ibid.

[5] Karl Kortum, "Notes on the Scows", National Maritime Museum.

[6] ibid.

[7] Boss, op. cit., p.114.

[8] Kortum, op. cit.

[9] Jack McNairn, in *Sea*, February 1955, p. 27.

[10] Robert D. Parmelee, *Pioneer Sonoma*. Sonoma: The Sonoma Valley Historical Society, 1972.

[11] Kortum, op. cit.

[12] ibid.

[13] Louis Green, "Sailing Vessels", in *Saga of Sonoma*. Sonoma: The Sonoma Valley Historical Society, 1976, p. 7-8.

[14] *List of Merchant Sailing Vessels of the U.S.*, p. 12, National Maritime Museum.

[15] California Historical Society, *Quarterly*, March 1938.

[16] Joe Vella, interview 1997.

[17] George Emanuels, *A Mid-California Illustrated History*, Walnut Creek, California, 1995.

[18] Robert Kiser, interview 1997.

[19] Charles Groskopf, interview 1997.

[20] *Master Carpenter's Certificate*, National Maritime Museum.

[21] *Merchant Steam Vessels of the United States*, p. 165, National Maritime Museum.

[22] Fred B. Duncan, *Deepwater Family*, Pantheon, n.d.

[23] Greg Jones, Jr., interview 1997.

[24] ibid.

[25] Sonoma Valley Historical Society, unidentified newspaper clipping, n.d.

[26] "Towed His Mate for 9 Miles", *Petaluma Argus*, September 7, 1900.

[27] *Sonoma Index-Tribune*, April 13, 1907.

Index